1,–

Renate Welsh
Little Vampie

Renate Welsh lebt als freie Schriftstellerin in Wien. Sie hat viele engagierte Kinder- und Jugendbücher geschrieben, für die sie neben anderen zahlreichen Auszeichnungen mehrfach den Österreichischen Staatspreis, den Preis der Stadt Wien und den Deutschen Jugendliteraturpreis erhielt. Ihr Gesamtwerk wurde 1995 mit dem Österreichischen Würdigungspreis und 2006 mit dem Literatur-Würdigungspreis des Landes Niederösterreich ausgezeichnet.

Weitere Titel von Renate Welsh bei dtv junior: siehe Seite 4

Heribert Schulmeyer wurde 1954 in Köln geboren. Er studierte an der ehemaligen Kölner Werkschule im Fachbereich Illustration und Freie Grafik und lebt heute als freier Illustrator in Köln.

Renate Welsh

Little Vampie

Mit Zeichnungen von Heribert Schulmeyer

Ins Englische übertragen von Anthea Bell

Mit Vokabelleisten von Birgit Hock

Deutscher Taschenbuch Verlag

Zu diesem Band (›Little Vampie‹) gibt es ein Unterrichtsmodell unter www.dtv.de/lehrer zum kostenlosen Download.

Eine englischsprachige Hörbuch-Ausgabe erscheint im Herbst 2007 bei Der Hörverlag, München. Die deutschsprachige Fassung (›Das Vamperl‹) ist dort ebenfalls erhältlich.

Von Renate Welsh sind außerdem bei dtv junior lieferbar:

Das Vamperl, dtv junior Lesebär 7562
Das Vamperl soll nicht alleine bleiben, dtv junior Lesebär 75016
Wiedersehen mit Vamperl, dtv junior Lesebär 75052
Das große Buch vom Vamperl, dtv junior 70730
Drachenflügel, dtv junior 70265
Sechs Streuner, dtv junior 70838
Schneckenhäuser, dtv pocket 78060
Das Gesicht im Spiegel, dtv pocket 78175

Originalausgabe
Juni 2007
Deutscher Taschenbuch Verlag GmbH & Co. KG, München
www.dtvjunior.de

Umschlagkonzept: Balk & Brumshagen
Umschlagbild: Heribert Schulmeyer
Gesetzt aus der Plantin 13/16,25'
Gesamtherstellung: Kösel, Krugzell
Gedruckt auf säurefreiem, chlorfrei gebleichtem Papier
Printed in Germany · ISBN 978-3-423-71236-1

Contents/Inhalt

Liebe Leserin, lieber Leser,

dieses Buch ist ein ganz besonderes englisches Buch, das Dir das Lesen in der Fremdsprache erleichtert:

- Auf jeder Seite im Text sind einige Wörter, manchmal auch ganze Sätze **fett** gedruckt. Das sind die Vokabeln und Redewendungen, die Du wahrscheinlich noch nicht kennst. Damit Du die Geschichte schnell lesen und gut verstehen kannst, ohne ständig jemanden fragen oder in einem Wörterbuch nachschauen zu müssen, gibt es unten auf jeder Seite Vokabelleisten. Die fett gedruckten Wörter sind dort ins Deutsche übersetzt, Du kannst sie beim Lesen einfach in Gedanken in die Geschichte einfügen.

- Bestimmt gibt es auch Vokabeln, die Du nicht kennst, die aber nicht fett gedruckt (und auch nicht übersetzt) sind. An diesen

Stellen kannst Du überlegen, ob es im Deutschen ein Wort gibt, das so ähnlich klingt. Versuch zu erraten, welches deutsche Wort an diese Stelle passt und lies einfach weiter. Du wirst der Geschichte bestimmt trotzdem folgen können!

Und nun: Lass Dich von Vampie, dem kleinen, ganz besonderen Vampir, mitnehmen ins Reich der Abenteuer! Viel Spaß!

Birgit Hock

A Surprise in a Cobweb

Mrs Lizzie's birth certificate said she was sixty-seven years old. But she didn't feel sixty-seven. »Except in my **joints,**« she sometimes said. »I feel ninety-seven in my joints. Particularly when the weather's on the change. But not otherwise, and the time between two birthdays is much too short anyway. How is anyone supposed to get used to the idea of being another year older so quickly?«

It was because of her joints that Mrs Lizzie had gone away **to stay at a health resort**.

Now she was walking upstairs. She had her travelling bag in one hand and a small case in the other.

cobweb: das Spinnennetz; **joints:** die Gelenke; **to stay at a health resort:** zur Kur sein

»These stairs haven't got any lower,« she **sighed**. She opened the door of her flat, put her bags down, and opened the window. Then she looked around her. There was **dust** everywhere. Three weeks' worth of dust. Mrs Lizzie rolled up her sleeves and began cleaning the flat. While she worked she sang:

»In dark ravines and ancient ruined halls
The night-owls fly, hooting tu-whit, tu-whoo.
Shiver, my friend within those haunted walls.
In search of blood, the vampire's after you.

Fair Adelaide was only seventeen.
She went by night into the woods alone.
Her love had left her, there among the green
Of nature she had gone to sigh and moan.

Then suddenly she heard a heartfelt plea:
›So sad and solitary, maiden fair?
Ah, would your tender heart but beat for me!
You'll be my queen if you my words will hear.

sighed: seufzte; **dust:** der Staub

I'd give you clothes of silk and velvet fine,
And never, never more would we two part.
You shall eat cake and drink the choicest wine.
If you will be the lady of my heart!‹

Poor girl, she stopped to listen to his wooing.
Oh Adelaide, why is your mouth so red?
Alas, alas, what is the vampire doing?
Before the sun sinks you'll lie pale and dead.«

Mrs Lizzie liked to sing while she worked. She had songs for hot days and songs for cold days. This was a song for hot days because it always gave her a cold **shiver** down her back.

»There we are, done!« said Mrs Lizzie. »And now I'll make myself a nice cup of coffee. The coffee at the health resort was the purest **dishwater**.«

Mrs Lizzie often talked to herself. She had lived alone ever since her mother died fifteen years before.

shiver: der Schauder; **dishwater:** das Spülwasser

While she put water in the coffee machine her eyes wandered around the kitchen. Then she saw the cobweb on the ceiling.
»Dear me, this won't do!« she said. »Not in my kitchen! It certainly is a particularly handsome cobweb, but it has no business here.«
She wrapped her **floor-cloth** round her **broom** and brushed the cobweb down. As she was about to shake out the floor-cloth she stopped in surprise. »No!« she said. »I don't believe it. This doesn't exist because it can't be true. And something that can't be true doesn't exist.«
She mopped the **perspiration** off her forehead. She cleaned her glasses and put them on again.
It really was there after all.
In the middle of the cobweb on her floor-cloth lay a **tiny** vampire, fast asleep.

floor-cloth: das Boden(putz)tuch; **broom:** der Besen; **perspiration:** der Schweiß; **tiny:** winzig

Mrs Lizzie took the floor-cloth between two fingers and put it on top of her **coal-box**.
The vampire went on sleeping.
There was a knock at the door of the flat.
Outside stood Mrs Anna, and behind her came her fox terrier Flocki.
»Good evening, Mrs Lizzie,« said Mrs Anna.
»How nice to see you home again. What was the resort like? Did it do you good?«
Flocki's nostrils widened. He pushed his way past Mrs Anna, put his tail between his legs, and started howling.
Mrs Lizzie stammered, »R-resort? What resort? Oh, the health resort …«
Flocki was howling so loudly that Mrs Anna couldn't hear a word anyway. She bent down, **patted** him, and said, »Flocki, how can you be so silly? This is Mrs Lizzie who always gives you such lovely bones! You know Mrs Lizzie, Flocki!«

coal-box: die Kohlenkiste; **patted:** tätschelte

Flocki only howled even louder. Mrs Anna was annoyed and then angry. »Stop it at once, will you, **you wretched animal**!«
When even that did no good, she raised a threatening hand. »You stupid dog! You just wait …«
»No!« said Mrs Lizzie. »Don't hit him! Flocki isn't stupid. In fact Flocki is a very clever dog.«
She went over to the coal-box.
»There, Mrs Anna, see for yourself!« And Mrs Lizzie folded back the corners of the floor-cloth.
Mrs Anna screamed.
Flocki pawed **frantically** at the front door of the flat, howling, barking and whining.
»Well, I must say …« cried Mrs Anna.
»Let's get Flocki out of here before you say anything!« cried Mrs Lizzie. »Otherwise the

you wretched animal: du Mistvieh; **frantically:** wie verrückt

noise will drive everyone in this building crazy!«
Mrs Anna shut Flocki up in her own flat. Then she came back and stood in the doorway with her arms folded.
»That's a vampire!« she said **sternly**.
»I thought so myself,« said Mrs Lizzie.
»So now what are we going to do?«
»I've no idea yet!«

sternly: streng

The little vampire sucked his vampire thumb. Mrs Anna shook herself. »Let's put it down the lavatory! And **flush** hard!« She was going to pick up the cloth.
Mrs Lizzie caught her arm. »No, don't do that! He's still so tiny.«
Mrs Anna looked Mrs Lizzie up and down. Then she shook her head.
»Well, throw him away in the **bin** if you have such a soft heart. But hurry up, because the **dustmen's truck** will be coming to collect the rubbish any moment now. And I wouldn't throw him away when the bin's empty. You never know. He might climb out again.«
»No,« said Mrs Lizzie. »That wouldn't be right. How can a vampire help being a vampire? I was scared myself at first. But just look at his tiny hands!«

flush: spüle (die Toilette); **bin:** die (Müll-)Tonne; **dustmen's truck:** die Müllabfuhr

Mrs Anna didn't want to look at his tiny hands or anything else about him. »I ask you, Mrs Lizzie! A vampire in our building! It's unthinkable. Just imagine: there you are asleep and he comes along and sucks your blood – down to the very last drop. By the time you wake up you'll have been dead for hours!«

The more Mrs Anna tried to talk her round, the more determined Mrs Lizzie was not to throw the little vampire away, either in the rubbish bin or down the loo. She was sorry she'd said anything at all. All she was thinking of was how **to get rid of** her neighbour.

»I'll do it for you,« Mrs Anna offered. »I always have to put spiders out because my husband is so scared of them. **You can't square this with your conscience.** If you're not

to get rid of: loswerden von; **you can't square this with your conscience:** Sie können das doch gar nicht verantworten

thinking of yourself, then think of the other **tenants**! What's more, you're so popular in the whole block of flats. We'd all miss you. And **wreaths** are terribly expensive at this time of year.«

Mrs Lizzie **glanced at** the little vampire. He wrinkled his nose in his sleep. It looked almost as if he were smiling.

»If you will excuse me now, Mrs Anna,« she said, »I'm tired after my **journey**. The doctor said it was **essential** for me to lie down when I feel tired.«

Shaking her head, Mrs Anna went away.

She was convinced that Mrs Lizzie couldn't be right in the head any more. She fetched Flocki, who was still whining, and took him for a walk. Then she came to a **decision**. She knocked at the door of the flat

tenants: die Mieter; **wreaths:** die Kränze; **glanced at:** warf einen Blick auf; **journey:** die Reise; **essential:** wichtig; **decision:** die Entscheidung

where her other neighbour, Mrs Maringer, lived.

Meanwhile Mrs Lizzie had been thinking hard.
The vampire is still tiny, she had thought. He doesn't know what blood tastes like yet. If I bring him up on milk he'll never get a taste for blood at all. **As you sow, so shall you reap**, that's what **my late granny** always said.
Mrs Lizzie covered the little vampire up with a handkerchief, went downstairs and bought a bottle of milk. Then she went to the toy-shop and bought a doll's feeding bottle.
Once she was home, she warmed the milk with a little sugar and poured it into the doll's bottle.

as you sow, so shall you reap: was du säst, das wirst du ernten; **my late granny:** meine Großmutter selig, d. h.: meine verstorbene Großmutter

The little vampire was just waking up. His **pointy** little mouth **screwed up**. He **squeaked** softly.
Carefully, Mrs Lizzie took him in her left hand. She put the **teat** of the bottle in his mouth with her right hand.
The little vampire **gulped** and smiled and gulped and smiled. Whenever he gulped he kicked his thin, hairy little legs. That **tickled** Mrs Lizzie's hand.
When the bottle was empty, the little vampire **burped**. Then he rolled up in Mrs Lizzie's hand and went to sleep again.
She wondered how she could make him a little bed.
She took her silver **necklace** out of its jewel box and put the little vampire inside on the sky-blue **cotton-wool**. Then she covered

pointy: spitz; **screwed up:** verzog sich; **squeaked:** fiepte; **teat:** Sauger; **gulped:** schluckte; **tickled:** kitzelte; **burped:** rülpste; **necklace:** die Halskette; **cotton-wool:** die Watte

him up with the handkerchief and put him on the living-room **window-sill** where the sun fell in.

window-sill: das Fensterbrett

A Cold Cup of Coffee

Mrs Lizzie was looking forward to her coffee. She took a cup out of the cupboard and put the sugar bowl on the kitchen table. Just then there was a knock on the door.

Mrs Anna and Mrs Maringer came in.

»I've just been making coffee,« said Mrs Lizzie. »Would you like some?«

Mrs Anna and Mrs Maringer looked at each other.

»No, thank you,« said Mrs Maringer sternly. »We have to talk to you.«

»You're welcome,« said Mrs Lizzie. She offered the two ladies chairs.

Mrs Anna was about to sit down, but Mrs Maringer shook her head. Mrs Anna straightened up again.

»You know the house rules?« asked Mrs Maringer.

»Of course I do,« said Mrs Lizzie. »If it's about

the cellar key, before I went away I gave it to …«
Mrs Anna interrupted her. »It's not about the cellar key.« Mrs Maringer cleared her throat. Mrs Anna said no more.
»You know that keeping pets is forbidden without special **permission** from the **owner** of the building, don't you?« said Mrs Maringer.
»Of course,« said Mrs Lizzie.
»And I expect you also know that **endangering** other tenants in any way whatsoever is strictly forbidden,« Mrs Maringer went on.
»Naturally,« said Mrs Lizzie. »Excuse me, I must shut the door. There's such a **draught** in here.« She closed the living-room door. Just don't start squeaking, she thought. She took a deep breath.

permission: die Erlaubnis; **owner:** der Besitzer; **endangering:** gefährden; **draught:** der Durchzug

»If it's about that little creature,« she began, »you can set your minds at rest.«
Mrs Anna sighed with relief. She turned to Mrs Maringer. »There, you see? I was against going to the police all along, but you always have **to wheel out the big guns** and make such a **fuss**!«
Mrs Maringer frowned. »What do you mean, me? You said you wouldn't be able to sleep a wink!«
The two ladies **looked daggers at each other**.
Mrs Maringer tapped her foot impatiently. Then she said, »And by the way, it's not so long ago since your beloved Flocki did his … well, you know what, outside my door!«
»My Flocki!« cried Mrs Anna **indignantly**. »You want to watch out for your Bello! Only

to wheel out the big guns: großes Geschütz auffahren; **fuss:** der Wirbel; **looked daggers at each other:** durchbohrten sich gegenseitig mit Blicken; **indignantly:** entrüstet

the other day he was showing his teeth and growling at my Flocki, and he scared the poor little thing so much that he fell three steps down the stairs. I had to take him to the **vet**!«

Both ladies **were** really **in their stride** now. Not until Mrs Lizzie tried to calm them down did they turn to her again.

»It was for your own sake, too,« said Mrs Anna. »I mean, we'd have been really sorry to lose you. You don't bear us a grudge, I hope?«

Mrs Maringer took a step forward. »And another thing I'd like to ask. How did you deal with … with the matter?«

Mrs Lizzie was on the point of throwing them out.

Then she thought: that will only mean more trouble.

vet: der Tierarzt (Kurzform von veterinarian);
were … in their stride: waren wütend

Mrs Maringer was looking expectant.
»Oh, stop that, do!« said Mrs Anna. »You can see you're upsetting Mrs Lizzie. The main thing is, she did it. It makes no difference whether she put the creature down the loo or in the bin, whether she **squashed** it or …«
»It makes a lot of difference, my dear Mrs Anna! It could have crept out of the dustmen's truck again. And then we'd be in fear of our lives!« Mrs Maringer took a step closer to Mrs Lizzie and looked deep into her eyes. »Tell me truthfully: did you throw it in the bin?«
»No,« said Mrs Lizzie.
And that was nothing but the truth.
At last the two ladies left.
Mrs Lizzie opened the living-room door again.
The little vampire had kicked the handkerchief off. Mrs Lizzie hoped he wasn't feeling

squashed: zerquetscht

cold. The sun wasn't shining on the window-sill any more.

The vampire's pointy nose began moving.

His hairy legs began kicking.

His hairy arms began flailing about.

Then the vampire squeaked. His squeak was not loud, but it was **penetrating**.

Mrs Lizzie hurried into the kitchen and filled the doll's bottle with milk. She put the teat in the vampire's mouth.

»Hush! Oh, for heaven's sake, keep quiet! It's important, understand? You simply have to understand! Even if you can't understand.«

She rocked the little vampire back and forth.

»I'm not at all sorry I told lies to those two. It's their own fault. You have to tell lies to people like that. You know, I'm a bit scared myself, little one. I wasn't prepared for some-

penetrating: durchdringend

one like you. But we'll manage between us, you and I. I just beg you, for goodness' sake keep quiet when there's someone else in the flat. No one must hear you. And most of all no one must see you. People have no idea what makes a vampire beautiful, understand? They think that only other people who look like them can be beautiful.«

Mrs Lizzie knew quite well that the little vampire couldn't understand her, but she talked to him all the same.
Who knows, she thought, perhaps he'll learn in time. After all, human babies don't understand a word at first, but all the same they like to hear someone talking to them.
She cut up an old handkerchief to make tiny **nappies** for the little vampire. She gave him the bottle.
When he was asleep again in his sky-blue cotton-wool bed, she thought she'd drink her coffee at long last.
The coffee was cold.
She didn't mind. They say that cold coffee makes you pretty. However, it bothered her that now there was skin on the milk she'd heated up. She hated skin on her milk.

nappies: die Windeln

»Just because those two are always **poking their noses into other people's business,**« she said **crossly**.
She fished the skin out of the pan of milk.
»Yuk!« she said. And with that she shook off the last of her **guilty conscience** for telling lies.
Skin on her milk! That was going too far.

poking their noses into other people's business: stecken ihre Nasen in die Angelegenheiten anderer Leute; **crossly:** verärgert; **guilty conscience:** ein schlechtes Gewissen

Learning to Fly and Other Skills

The vampire grew fast.
After a week the jewel box was too small for him.
After two weeks the button box was too small for him.
Mrs Lizzie knitted a coloured blanket out of left-over wool and made him a bed in her sewing basket.
He could hold his own bottle when he drank milk now.

He was using the box of **wood-shavings** that Mrs Lizzie had put in the loo for him.

skills: die Kunstfertigkeiten; **wood-shavings:** die Sägespäne

He tilted his head on one side when she talked to him. He was listening to her. Sometimes he squeaked softly, and it sounded like an answer.
Mrs Lizzie left the radio on all the time now.
Better safe than sorry, she told herself. If the neighbours do hear anything, I can always say it was the radio.
She hurried when she went shopping. She was afraid the vampire might get up to something while she was out.
The woman in the **dairy**, the **greengrocer**, the butcher and the newsagent were surprised that Mrs Lizzie had no time for a nice **chat** any more.

better safe than sorry: sicher ist sicher; **dairy:** der Milchladen; **greengrocer:** der Gemüseladen; **chat:** das Schwätzchen

The little vampire liked sitting on the window-sill and looking out at the street.
He climbed the curtains and swung from the **curtain cord**.
He sat on Mrs Lizzie's shoulder when she was cooking.
Sometimes he squeaked in her ear. It tickled.
Once it tickled so much that she dropped her cooking spoon in the tomato soup, and then Mrs Lizzie and the little vampire were covered with red spots. It looked as if they had measles. Or **scarlet fever**.
In his third week the vampire made his first attempts to fly. He climbed on the kitchen chair.
He spread his big, thin wings. They **rustled** like **tissue paper.**

curtain cord: die Vorhangschnur; **scarlet fever:** Scharlach; **rustled:** knisterten; **tissue paper:** das Seidenpapier

He flapped his wings a couple of times, and then he jumped.
As he dropped, he forgot to beat his wings and landed on his tummy.
He squeaked **pitifully**.
Mrs Lizzie came running out of the living-

pitifully: kläglich

room. She picked him up. She stroked him and **comforted** him.
She felt his arms and legs.
»Nothing broken,« she said with relief. She made him some **camomile tea** to **calm** him **down**.
The vampire didn't like camomile tea. He blew it out of his pointy **muzzle**. Mrs Lizzie's glasses were sprayed all over and could have done with **windscreen wipers**.
»Off you go to bed!« she **scolded** him. She carried him into the living-room and went back to the kitchen, where by now the milk had boiled over. Five minutes later he made his second attempt at flying. This time he took off from the window-sill. And this time it went much better.
When Mrs Lizzie came in again he flew at

comforted: tröstete; **camomile tea:** der Kamillentee; **calm down:** beruhigen; **muzzle:** die Schnauze; **windscreen wipers:** die Scheibenwischer; **scolded:** schimpfte

her head. She had a terrible shock and screamed. The little vampire lovingly **ruffled** her hair.

One Sunday morning Mrs Lizzie heard shouting on the stairs. For goodness' sake, she wondered, what's happened? She opened the front door of her flat.

Mrs Miller on the third floor was scolding her son Hannes.

He had been to see his granny, and she had given him a basket of apples. On the way home he had passed a playground where his friends were playing football.

»Hannes!« they shouted. »The other side's leading three-one! Come on!«

Hannes put the basket down and joined in the game. He didn't stop to think that he was wearing his best trousers.

Now there was a hole in the trousers and a large grass stain on them.

ruffled: zerzauste

»Come here, will you?« shouted Mrs Miller. »Come here so that I can **give you some stick**! As you richly deserve. How often have I told you to look after your clothes? I suppose you think money grows on trees? You'll soon see what grows on trees!«
Hannes started crying. The basket fell over. Apples bumped noisily down the stairs.
»I'll give you something to cry about! Come here, I said!« And Mrs Miller swung her arm back.
Mrs Lizzie was going to remind her that children think differently from grown-ups, and Hannes hadn't meant to do anything wrong. But just as she was opening her mouth the vampire **flitted** past her. Now everything happened very fast.
The vampire **clambered up** the **banisters**

give you some stick: dir eine Tracht Prügel geben; **flitted:** huschte; **clambered up:** kletterte hinauf; **banister:** das Geländer

to the third floor. He fluttered past Hannes. He was flying straight for Mrs Miller, aiming for her stomach.
Mrs Lizzie felt quite sick with fear. She closed her eyes.

She didn't want to see **what was bound to happen** next.

»Ow! Something stung me!« cried Mrs Miller. »Are there wasps in this block of flats?«

Mrs Lizzie blinked.

She saw the vampire beating his wings as he **hovered** in the air in front of Mrs Miller's stomach. Right in front of her **gall bladder**. Mrs Lizzie knew exactly where the gall bladder was. She'd had an operation on hers a year ago.

Now the vampire took his sharp little muzzle out of Mrs Miller's gall bladder. Mrs Miller dropped her arm.

The vampire turned in the air and flew back to Mrs Lizzie's flat.

Mrs Miller ran her hand through Hannes' hair. »My word, do you know what you look

what was bound to happen: was kommen musste; **hovered:** flatterte; **gall bladder:** die Gallenblase

like? Like the **goalie** after an international played in the rain!«

Hannes stared open-mouthed at his mother.

She smiled. »Well, so who won?«

»Who … wh … what?«

»Who won? Your football game, of course,« said his mother. »What else? What's the matter with you, don't you feel well?«

Hannes slowly closed his mouth again. He shook his hair back from his forehead.

»We won!« he said. »And I shot the last goal. It was a solo run!«

Hannes **thrust out his chest**, stuck both thumbs into his **braces**, and **twanged them**.

Mrs Miller put her arm round his shoulders, and they both went back to their flat. The Millers' front door closed.

goalie: der Torhüter; **thrust out his chest:** streckte seine Brust heraus; **braces:** die Hosenträger; **twanged them:** ließ sie (= die Hosenträger) schnalzen

Mrs Lizzie went back to her own flat, too. Only now did she notice how badly her knees were shaking. She had to sit down. The little vampire flew up to sit on her **lap**.

»You're not a vampire at all,« she said. »A vampire sucks people's blood. But you suck out their **bad temper**! Do you know what you are? You're a vampie, a dear little vampie.«

He bounced up and down on her knees.

»But oh, what a fright you gave me!« she said. »I thought my heart would stop, I was so scared.«

The little vampire **snuggled** close to her. »I just wish I knew how it works,« she murmured.

Little Vampie patted his fat little tummy with both hands and smacked his lips. »Why, of course! You sucked the **poison** out of her gall

lap: der Schoß; **bad temper:** die schlechte Laune, hier: die Bosheit; **snuggled:** schmiegte sich an; **poison:** das Gift

bladder – the stuff that people call the **gall** or **bile** – and then she suddenly realized that things weren't nearly as bad as she thought. Was that it?«

Little Vampie nodded eagerly, and turned a few **somersaults**.

gall/bile: die Gallenflüssigkeit; **somersaults:** die Purzelbäume

Mrs Lizzie remembered how surprised Hannes had looked. »He just couldn't believe his mother was suddenly being so nice to him!« She laughed.
Then she turned serious. »But suppose she'd seen you? You must be careful, little one. You must be very, very careful. You see, Little Vampie, if people feel scared they don't know what they're doing any more.«
Little Vampie rubbed his pointy little vampire muzzle against her big round human nose.
»And when I think,« said Mrs Lizzie, »when I think how many people could do with having the poison sucked out of their gall bladders ...«
Little Vampie happily squeaked **agreement** into her ear. That evening Mrs Lizzie sang her Little Vampie a song:

agreement: das Einverständnis

»A vampire need not
Be a really bad lot!
Rear him gently, be kind,
And you'll very soon find
He responds like a shot.

My Little Vampie just drinks milk, he never touches blood,
He seeks out nasty people and soon he's made them good.
When someone is furious and stamps on the ground,
Up flies Little Vampie with never a sound,
And as the cross person gets madder and madder,
Vampie sucks up the poison from in his gall bladder.
My Little Vampie just drinks milk, he never touches blood,
He seeks out nasty people and soon he's made them good.«

Vampie Out and About

Two days later Mrs Lizzie had to go shopping again. She had a hard time of it carrying a heavy shopping bag full of food for a whole week.

She put the bag down on the low wall outside the park to have a little rest.

There were eight children in the park standing in a circle around a boy. Mrs Lizzie knew him. He lived with his grandmother. He was bottom of the class at school, and always walked with his shoulders slightly **hunched**.

hunched: gebeugt, gebückt

Among the other children Mrs Lizzie **recognized** Hannes, Klaus and Karin. The children were chanting:

»Ha, ha, ha, ho, ho, hum!
Dieter here is really dumb!
Ha, ha, ha, ho, ho, hummer,
Dieter here is even dumber.
Stupid at home, stupid at school,
Dieter is a silly fool.

Ha, ha, ha, ho, ho, ho!
Dieter is a hunchback, so –
Ha, ha, ha, ho, ho, ho –
Crookback Dieter must lie low.
Dieter's back is bent and wonky,
Dieter is a silly donkey.«

And they were laughing while they sang. Dieter stood in the middle of the circle, trying to shrink as small as he could.
»What are you?« asked Klaus.
Dieter hunched his shoulders and ducked his head down between them. Now he really did look like a **hunchback**.

recognized: erkannte; **hunchback:** der Bucklige

»You're **dumb**!« everyone shouted.
Shall I say something, Mrs Lizzie wondered, or would I just be making things worse for the poor boy?
Now Karin was asking, »What is he?«

dumb: dumm, doof

They all cried in chorus, »He's a hunchback!«

Suddenly Klaus **screeched**. But only for a moment.

Karin pointed to Dieter and asked again, »What is he?«

Before the others could answer, Klaus called, »He's not dumb! We're the ones being dumb!«

»Klaus is **round the bend**,« said Karin. »**He must have a screw loose**.«

»It's mean for us all to gang up on one person,« said Klaus.

»It doesn't bother Dieter,« said Karin. »He doesn't understand anyway.«

»Yes, he does,« said Hannes. »He understands perfectly well.«

Dieter said nothing.

screeched: kreischte; **round the bend:** übergeschnappt; **he must have a screw loose:** bei dem ist wohl eine Schraube locker

Then Karin screeched.
She rubbed her eyes with both hands. Then she went up to Dieter. He raised his arms **to protect** his face.
»Would you like to come round to my place this afternoon?« asked Karin. »We could do our homework together.«
Dieter **peeped out** from behind his elbows.
»Or I know what, come home with me now,« said Karin. »There's spaghetti and cheese with salad for lunch. You can tell your grandmother.«
Dieter slowly lowered his arms.
»My grandmother's at work,« he **muttered**.
»Then we can go straight away.«
Karin put out her hand to him. Dieter hesitated.
»But you must come to my place tomorrow,« said Klaus.

to protect: schützen; **peeped out:** guckte heraus; **muttered:** murmelte

»And mine the day after,« said Hannes.
Karin took Dieter's hand, and he let her lead him away.
Mrs Lizzie ran home as fast as she could go.

Little Vampie was sitting on the window-sill biting his nails.
He hated it when Mrs Lizzie cut his finger-nails.
»Listen, Little Vampie ...«
He looked at her very **innocently** – too innocently. It stuck out a mile.
»I told you how dangerous it is for people to see you, didn't I?« Mrs Lizzie scolded him. »Will you never learn?«
Little Vampie hung his head.
He screwed up his vampire muzzle into a sad **pout**. Mrs Lizzie sighed.
»Well, I agree, it's nice for the children to help

innocently: unschuldig; **pout:** die Schnute

poor Dieter. It really is! I was just wondering if there wasn't something I could do myself when … when you came along. But you don't know what our dear neighbours would like to do to you.« She stroked his pointy vampire ears with one finger. »Don't go flying off on your own, at least. Wait till I'm there. Otherwise goodness knows what might happen!«
Mrs Lizzie blew her nose.
»I know, I know. At my age a person ought not to be having any more children. Not even vampire children.«
Little Vampie let a big tear drop down the neck of her dress.
»Oh, this is too much! Now I have **to comfort** *you* for being so **naughty**!« said Mrs Lizzie.

to comfort: trösten; **naughty:** unartig

Danger!

However hard Mrs Lizzie tried to keep Little Vampie in the house, **it was no good**.
As soon as he heard car **horns** hooting angrily down in the street he was off.
There were traffic jams every morning. The drivers couldn't move their cars either forward or back. They **cursed** and **swore**.

it was no good: es nützte nichts; **horn:** die Hupe; **cursed:** fluchten; **swore:** schimpften

No one wanted to give way to anyone else. Until Little Vampie stepped in.
One sting – and he was sucking poison from a **furious** driver's gall bladder. Another sting, and a second driver was smiling, with no idea what had happened to him.
»Good morning,« said the first driver.
»Good morning,« said the second driver.
»After you,« said the first driver.
»No, no, do go first,« said the second driver.
The policeman on the corner had his notebook in his hand and was turning it this way and that. Now he put it back in his pocket.
That corner had once been **the worst** traffic **black spot** in the whole town, the place where most accidents happened.
Now the policeman sometimes wondered why he was standing there at all. You didn't need traffic lights for such polite drivers, you

furious: wütend; **the worst ... black spot:** die schlimmste Ecke

didn't need policemen. The chaos sorted itself out. The stream of traffic flowed as calmly as a **brook** running through a meadow. The policeman didn't even have to hold up cars at the road junction to let the schoolchildren **cross**. Drivers stopped **of their own accord**, or so at least it seemed to the policeman. He had no idea that it was all Little Vampie's work.

Mrs Lizzie stood at the window watching. She always found herself **gasping for air** when he stung someone.

And when he came back and saw how worried she was, he looked guilty. He put his head on one side and snuggled into the **hollow** of her **throat**.

brook: der Bach; **(to) cross:** die Straße überqueren; **of their own accord:** aus eigenem Antrieb; **gasping for air:** nach Luft schnappen; **hollow:** die Grube; **throat:** der Hals, die Kehle

But next time car horns hooted he was off again. He could squeeze through the narrowest of **cracks**.

Mrs Lizzie was beginning to realize that she couldn't keep him shut in. She always scolded a little when he came back, out of habit, but at the same time she was **proud** of him.

Every evening she sang him the song she had made up for him:

»Little Vampie wakes at dawn,
Rises bright and early.
Down he flies into the street with all its hurly-burly.
Where people quarrel, scuffle and fight
All about nothing, dear me, what a sight!
They shout and scream, they're mean and they're vile,
Until Little Vampie sucks out their bile.
My Vampie just drinks milk, he never touches blood,
He seeks out nasty people and soon he's made them good.
When the cars are all racing as if they were chasing
People crossing the street who are made to retreat,
And drivers lose patience and turn up the heat,
When you hear the loud sound
Of horns hooting all round,

cracks: die Ritzen; **proud:** stolz

When everyone's angry and everyone's wrong,
Then my Little Vampie comes flying along.
He sucks out their gall,
And settles it all!
See how it goes now!
The angry drivers stop driving so blindly,
They smile and wave, they give way kindly.
They don't know what makes them feel not so sore,
But they're nicer to others than ever before.
My Little Vampie just drinks milk, he never touches blood,
He seeks out nasty people and soon he's made them good.«

Little Vampie wouldn't go to sleep until she had sung the song. Then she stood by his basket for a while looking at him. She stroked his hairy head and his hairy hands, and then she covered him up.

One sunny afternoon Little Vampie was sitting quietly beside Mrs Lizzie at the open window. Whenever someone looked up from the street he hid behind her **stout** arms.

»I wonder who that **shady character** is?« asked Mrs Lizzie, pointing to a man who was

stout: kräftig; **shady character:** der Finsterling

peering up and down the street before **slinking** into the building opposite. »I'm sure he has no good in mind.«

Then she clapped her hand over her mouth. I never ought to have said that, she thought. But it was already far too late. Little Vampie had shot out of the window, fluttered across the street, and disappeared into the block of flats opposite.

slinking: schleichen

Mrs Lizzie fetched her opera glasses and kept watch.
Little Vampie found the stranger on the third floor of the building opposite. He was just opening the front door of a flat with a **skeleton key**. Little Vampie didn't know that it was a skeleton key, but he could smell the poison in the strange man's gall bladder.
He stung him, and began to suck.
But the man caught Little Vampie by one wing before he had sucked out enough poison. With the last of his strength he took one more deep **gulp**, and then he had to let go. He fell down the stairs. His wing was torn. He **dragged** himself to the front door of the building, and **collapsed** on the step outside it.
Mrs Lizzie saw him fall and ran down. It was years since she had run so fast.

skeleton key: der Dietrich; **gulp:** der Schluck; **dragged:** schleppte; **collapsed:** brach zusammen

All the same, she was nearly too late. Bello was already sniffing Little Vampie, nudging him back and forth with his doggy nose.
»Get away!« shouted Mrs Lizzie.
Bello growled and snapped at Little Vampie.
Mrs Lizzie pushed Bello aside, picked Little Vampie up, and carried him home. He didn't move.
She sat down in the kitchen and put the little vampire on her lap. There were tears running down her **cheeks**. One of them fell on the little vampire's muzzle. He **twitched**, and then he **licked** the tear away. »You're alive!« cried Mrs Lizzie. »You're alive!«
With trembling fingers, she felt his wing. When she found the break in it she cried again. Then she fetched some toothpicks and **sticking plaster**.

cheeks: die Wangen; **twitched:** zuckte; **licked:** leckte; **sticking plaster:** Heftpflaster

»You're not going to like this,« she said. »But it has to be done. After all, you want to be able to fly again.«
She filled a **thimble** with rum.
»Drink this. Then it won't hurt so much when I set your wing for you.«
Little Vampie **shuddered**, but he drank it.
Mrs Lizzie **splinted** his wing with five toothpicks, and stuck them in place with sticking plaster.
She wasn't to know what was happening meanwhile in the block of flats opposite. The man she had seen was standing in the strange flat, but he couldn't remember what he had come here for.
The flat belonged to an old lady.
»Is there someone there?« the old lady called from her bedroom.
»Yes, it's me,« he replied without thinking.

thimble: der Fingerhut; **shuddered:** schüttelte sich; **splinted:** schiente

»What are you doing here?« asked the old lady.
»Well, I was really going to steal your money,« he said. »Or your jewellery. But now I don't feel like stealing your things any more, I've no idea why.«
»So you're a **burglar**,« said the old lady. »You should be ashamed of yourself.«
»It's so long since I felt ashamed of myself that I'm not sure if I can still do it,« he said. »But **I'll have a go**.«
»I tell you what,« said the old lady, »if you're still there, you could go shopping for me. I've been in bed ill for a week, my **fridge** is empty and I'm hungry.«
So the burglar went shopping for the old lady. He carried her full **rubbish bin** downstairs. He even went round the flat with the vacuum

burglar: der Einbrecher; **I'll have a go:** ich werde es versuchen; **fridge:** der Kühlschrank; **rubbish bin:** der Mülleimer

cleaner. And he kept shaking his head the whole time. This wasn't like him at all.

Later on, the burglar and the old lady ate **supper** together.

»What do you earn in your trade?« asked the old lady.

»Times are bad,« he said. »Particularly when you're working on your own. I can't pick modern security locks with my skeleton key. And I'm not as young as I was.«

supper: das Abendessen

The old lady nodded, and praised his chicken soup.
Later she made him an offer. »Come and see me every day. I can't pay you much because I don't have much. It wouldn't have been worth your while to steal from me, but if you'll come and cook for me you'll make an honest living. And you won't have to fear the police.«
»You won't have to fear burglars either,« he said, and laughed. »**I know that lot**. They won't have a chance with me around.«
If Mrs Lizzie had known all this it would have been a comfort to her. Particularly if she had guessed that the burglar would **nurse the old lady back to health**. And next summer the two of them are even going to Venice, because the old lady wants to go for a ride in

I know that lot: ich kenne die Brüder; **(to) nurse the old lady back to health:** die alte Frau gesund pflegen;

a gondola just once. The **former** burglar thinks there are too many **pigeons** and too many thieves in Venice, but the old lady insists on having her way. However, there's still a long time to go before next summer.

former: ehemalig; **pigeons:** die Tauben

Camomile Tea and Boredom

In the evening Little Vampie ran a temperature.

Mrs Lizzie put cold **compresses** round his hot head.

She dipped two of his nappies in **vinegar** and water and wrapped them round his hot feet.

She poured cool camomile tea into his mouth.

She held his hot hand.

She **soothed** him when he began kicking about in his fever.

She swallowed her tears.

His fever got worse and worse. Little Vampie lay there under his brightly coloured blanket with his eyes closed. Now and then he opened them very wide and trembled.

boredom: die Langeweile; **compresses:** die Umschläge; **vinegar:** der Essig; **soothed:** beruhigte

»I'm here with you,« said Mrs Lizzie, but she realized that he didn't understand her.

After midnight his temperature dropped.

Little Vampie fell asleep.

Mrs Lizzie sat beside his basket keeping watch.

Little Vampie slept until twelve noon next day. When he finally woke up he wasn't feverish any more. But he was still very weak. Mrs Lizzie had to pick him up and put

him on his box of shavings. He squeaked pitifully if she went out of the living-room for a few minutes.

Little Vampie soon got better, but he couldn't move very well with the toothpicks splinting his wing.
»Keep still, do!« said Mrs Lizzie.
She said it as regularly as the **pendulum clock** in the living-room struck the hours.
Little Vampie was in a bad temper.
Whenever a car hooted in the street below, he **fidgeted**. Whenever he heard Mrs Miller scolding on the stairs he complained. Whenever he heard dogs barking **he was all on edge**.
It was a difficult time for Mrs Lizzie. She tried to entertain Little Vampie. She sang to him until she was **hoarse**.

pendulum clock: die Pendeluhr; **fidgeted:** zappelte; **he was all on edge:** er wurde ganz nervös; **hoarse:** heiser

He didn't want to play **Snakes and Ladders**, or **Nine Men's Morris**, or **Snatch the Hat.** He kicked the **dominoes** around.
»**My patience is wearing thin**,« said Mrs Lizzie. »This is all very well, but whose fault is your broken wing, yours or mine?«
Then Little Vampie looked **guilty** and buried his pointed muzzle in the hollow of Mrs Lizzie's hand.

Snakes and Ladders: das Leiterspiel; **Nine Men's Morris:** das Mühlespiel; **Snatch the Hat:** Fang den Hut; **dominoes:** die Dominosteine; **my patience is wearing thin:** jetzt reißt mir aber gleich der Geduldsfaden; **guilty:** schuldbewusst

That always stopped her feeling cross.
But soon afterwards it all began again.
At the end of the first week after breaking his wing, Little Vampie was lying on the window-sill in his basket.
The sun was shining.
Mrs Lizzie was doing her ironing.
Suddenly Little Vampie gave a loud squeak and waved his arms about.
Mrs Lizzie ran to the window.
In the block of flats opposite, the old lady and the former burglar were peacefully leaning out of their own window side by side, looking down at the street.
Little Vampie clapped his hands.
Mrs Lizzie patted his head.
»So it wasn't all for nothing after all. That's good. That's very good, my dear.«
Little Vampie squeaked enthusiastically. He hopped about in his basket with **delight**

delight: die Freude

until Mrs Lizzie was afraid he would tip over, basket and all, and fall off the sill.

That day Mrs Lizzie went shopping for the first time since the accident. She had no food at all left in the house. For the last three days she had eaten nothing but porridge. On the way home she bought a newspaper. When she sat down to read it, Little Vampie looked **pathetic** until she read it aloud to him.

Then he lay there perfectly still, listening hard.

Mrs Lizzie wondered if it was good for him. She thought there was a lot in the newspaper that was unsuitable for children. Including vampire children. But then she thought: who knows how much he understands? No more than is good for him, I'm sure. His eyes are so clever. If only he could talk!

From now on Mrs Lizzie had to buy a newspaper every day. When she had finished read-

pathetic: mitleiderregend

ing it aloud she **recited** poetry to Little Vampie. She was surprised to find how many poems she still knew by heart.
After two weeks Mrs Lizzie was able to take the strips of sticking plaster off.
Little Vampie squeaked and trembled.
»What must be, must be,« said Mrs Lizzie, removing the toothpicks.
»It looks as good as new,« she said, delighted. »But do be careful!« Little Vampie was flapping his wings gently up and down.
On his first **trial** flight next day he **reeled** all over the flat, flying through the air **at an odd angle**.

recited: sagte auf; **trial:** der Versuch; **reeled:** torkelte; **at an odd angle:** in einem schiefen Winkel

Two days later, however, he was flying almost as well as before. Only not quite so fast.

»But you're not flying away from me on your own again!« said Mrs Lizzie sternly.

No Cycling

Saturday was a wonderful day. Mrs Lizzie thought it would do Little Vampie good to get some **proper** fresh air.
After lunch she spread a soft towel in her big shopping bag. Then she put the little vampire on the towel. He kicked and struggled.
»Oh, I see what it is,« said Mrs Lizzie. »You're annoyed because you can't see anything.«
She took him out and cut a **peephole** in her good shopping bag. Little Vampie was **satisfied** now. He let her take him for a walk down the high street, across the park and through the housing estate.
They came to the playground.
Three small children were sitting in the sand-

proper: richtig; **peephole:** das Guckloch; **satisfied:** zufrieden

box building a sand castle. Mrs Lizzie sat down on the bench and watched them. She was tired, her joints were aching again, and she liked watching children.

Another crowd of children came riding up on their bicycles.

They cycled round the playground in a circle.

They had a race.

They had a slalom.

When they were having a competition to see who could cycle most slowly the **caretaker** came along. »Stop that at once!« he cried. »No cycling in the playground!«

»But where are we to ride our bikes, then?« asked one girl.

The caretaker waved his arms about. »**Cheeky, too**! Can't you read? What do they teach

caretaker: der Hausmeister; **cheeky, too:** auch noch frech werden

you kids these days?« He took the girl by the shoulders and led her up to a big notice. »What does that say? It says ›No Cycling‹, plain and clear. So off you go! If you don't get out at once, you and your bikes, I'm going to call the management of the block.«
A smaller child fell off his bike and began to cry. Mrs Lizzie held her bag tight with both hands. But it was too late. Little Vampie had already fluttered out. He was making for the caretaker's stomach.
He bit.
He began sucking.
The caretaker **scratched** the back of his head. Then he said, »Well, yes – where else *are* they to ride their bikes?«
The children stood perfectly still. The little boy stopped crying.
»They can't cycle in the street because they're

scratched: kratzte

still too small,« the caretaker went on. »If they cycle on the pavement they might knock down children and old people. So where can they take their bikes? You can't ride a bike round the kitchen.« He turned to the children, looking stern. »All right, then. Ride your bikes here. But mind you're careful!«

He picked up his big broom and went away. The children stared at him. »What got into *him* all of a sudden?« asked one boy.

The little boy who had fallen off his bike said, »A **bat** got into him. I saw it.«

»**Don't tell fibs**, Oliver,« said a girl. »The stories you think up!«

»I did see it,« insisted Oliver. »It was a beautiful bat.«

Mrs Lizzie held her bag tight and quickly went home.

bat: die Fledermaus; **don't tell fibs:** erzähl doch keine Märchen

»Little Vampie,« she said, »you'd turn my hair grey if it wasn't grey already.«
Little Vampie smacked his lips and rubbed his round little tummy.

Mrs Lizzie sighed.
»I'd have thought you'd be more careful after your accident. But no! Quite the opposite. Before your accident at least you stayed near home.«
Little Vampie looked at her with his head on one side.
His eyes went large and round when she talked to him.
He **burrowed** his nose into her hand.
But he always flew away again.
Sometimes Mrs Lizzie found out about it by chance.
Sometimes she didn't.
That was just as well, or she would have been even more upset.
She was upset all the time anyway.

burrowed: grub

She never found out, for instance, about the day when Little Vampie flew after Hannes and went to school.

Little Vampie hid behind the blackboard.

During the lesson when the children did sums in an arithmetic test he went to sleep.

When the children read out loud he dozed.

When the children drew he would have liked to fly round the classroom looking at all the pretty pictures. Specially the jungle pictures.

When the last lesson came and the children were running about and yawning and talking, the teacher was cross.

»Get your exercise books out!« he said.

Little Vampie flitted out from behind the blackboard and sucked a little poison from the teacher's gall bladder.

The teacher ran all his fingers through his hair.

»It looks to me as if you're tired,« he said. »Why don't I tell you a funny story instead? How about that?«

All the children sat there open-mouthed.
Hannes almost swallowed a fly.
The teacher began. »An elephant was marching through the jungle ...«
»Please, there's a bat here!« cried a girl.
Little Vampie shot out through the open window, settled on a window-sill, and waved to the little girl.
He hadn't expected to find two pigeons

perching on the window-sill, too. They began **cooing** loudly. Little Vampie made himself look very small. The pigeons excitedly tripped back and forth. Next moment there was a whirring in the air. A whole flock of pigeons came down. Beaks pecked at the little vampire. Round eyes sparkled at him. But at the last moment he managed to spread his wings. He was in luck. A light wind carried him away.

That afternoon Little Vampie stayed at home with Mrs Lizzie. He settled comfortably in the hollow of her throat.
Now and then she put her head on one side as she was reading and stroked his tummy with her chin. Then he squeaked softly and happily. But next day he was out and about again.
There wasn't much going on today at the

perching: hocken; **cooing:** gurren

road junction. Friendliness had become almost second nature to the drivers who passed this way daily. Little Vampie helped himself to a little breakfast of bile from a married couple who were drinking coffee by their open window.

»You've gone and **dented** my car again!« said the husband angrily.

dented: verbeult

»*Your* car?« cried his wife. »I thought it was *our* car!«
»Just because you can't drive properly,« the man went on. »Women are bad drivers.«
His wife made a face. »I'm sure the car got that dent yesterday evening when you …«
»When I …?« The man went red as a beetroot. »Trying to blame me for it, are you?«
Little Vampie bit him first and then her. When he flew on, the husband was washing up the coffee cups and his wife was drying them. And they were laughing. Little Vampie saw the children on their way to school. Hannes and Dieter were taking turns kicking a fir-cone ahead of them.
Little Vampie kept his distance. He'd already been seen twice by a child. No grown-ups had ever spotted him yet.
He came to a part of town that was quite new to him. He heard pounding, booming noises behind a high wall. He flew over the wall. There was a large building behind it. Little

Vampie looked through one of the windows. He saw several different machines standing in a large **shed**. **Levers** were going up and down, gigantic blocks were thumping down on metal.
Little Vampie was scared. The booming shook him back and forth, although he was clinging to the window.
He flew to the next shed. There were no noisy machines here. Loud music was playing instead.
A **conveyor belt** ran right down the shed, moving all the time. Shiny silver boxes moved along it.
Women stood beside the conveyor belt. They were all wearing **scarves** on their heads.
One woman screwed two screws into each box.
The next woman twisted a knob into it.

shed: die Halle; **levers:** die Hebel; **conveyor belt:** das Fließband; **scarves:** die Kopftücher

The woman next to her **fitted a spring**.
One woman had a red nose. She kept blowing it.
Once she reached for her handkerchief, and then she had to run to catch up with the belt because one of the boxes had moved past her.
A man came up to her.
»If you carry on like that you'll be fired,« he said. »You've missed putting in six screws today already.«
»I have such a bad cold,« said the woman.
»I'm not interested in your cold,« said the man. »Now you've missed another two. Go and get your papers!«
»Are you really firing me?« asked the woman, horrified.
»You bet I'm firing you!« said the man.
Little Vampie flew into the shed. He stung the man and began sucking.

fitted a spring: befestigte eine Feder

Such a huge wave of bile came out all at once that Little Vampie **choked**. His throat was burning. He almost let go. But he saw the woman's desperate face and went on sucking.
The man looked round the shed as if he were seeing it for the first time.
»It looks to me,« he said, »as if we've set the conveyor belt to go too fast. You can't even stop to blow your nose!« He went over to a **switchbox** and pressed two knobs.
The conveyor belt ran more slowly. The women looked at each other in surprise.
»Now, you go off to the canteen,« the man said to the woman with the red nose, »and get yourself a nice hot cup of tea. I'll take over here while you drink it.«
The woman didn't move.

choked: verschluckte sich; **switchbox:** der Schaltkasten

»Go on, what are you waiting for?« asked the man.

Little Vampie felt pressure in his stomach. He had drunk far too much bile. He could hardly fly with that fat, heavy tummy. He almost stuck in the half-open window.

On the way home he met two girls making fun of an old woman. He would have liked to do something about it, but he really was too full.

There was no room left inside him for even the tiniest little **sip**.

Mrs Lizzie immediately noticed that he was sad. She saw his **bulging** tummy. »You've been overdoing things, haven't you?« she said. »I can well imagine it.« She warmed one of his old nappies and put it on his tummy. Then she sat in her armchair and took him on her lap.

»To think how much poisonous bile and gall there is in the world! You could suck it out until you were blue in the face, and no one would notice that anything much had gone. Well, Hannes notices, of course. And the old lady who lives opposite. But two blocks away they hardly notice a thing, do they? One Little Vampie can't do it all by himself.«

They sat quietly there for a while. Then Mrs Lizzie smiled.

sip: der Schluck; **bulging:** prallvoll

»Listen,« she said. »I've thought of something.«
She sang him a new song.

»Little Vampie wakes at dawn,
Rises bright and early.
Down he flies into the street with all its hurly-burly,
Where he's always meeting folk
So full of bile it makes you choke.
But even if he stung all day
He couldn't suck so much away.
He's very small, he's on his own,
He cannot do it all alone.
We need more Vampies, nine or ten,
We'd better search for some, and then
Wherever those vampires may happen to hide
I'm sure that we'll find them, whatever betide!
For ten little vampires we'll go on our quest,
So that my Little Vampie can soon have a rest.«

A Difficult Decision

Next morning Mrs Lizzie put on her comfortable shoes. She packed up some sandwiches.

Little Vampie was flying round the flat, squeaking with excitement.

Mrs Lizzie thought: what have I gone and promised? Where do we even begin to look? I'd almost rather it was pouring with rain. Then I'd have another day to think about it. But I'm sure it's not going to rain today. Or tomorrow either. I can feel it in my joints. That's to say, I don't feel them aching, so it can't be going to rain.

She said out loud, »Stop fidgeting and drink your milk! We want to make an early start.«

Little Vampie spilled half his thimbleful of milk. That hadn't happened for a long time.

Mrs Lizzie put on her prettiest hat. She had bought it ten or twelve years ago when her

niece **got married**. Perhaps a **wedding hat** will bring luck, she thought. We can do with some luck.
The main thing, however, was that Little Vampie could sit under it and see through the weave of the straw.

got married: geheiratet hatte; **wedding hat:** der Hochzeitshut

»Don't dance about like that. You're messing up my hair,« said Mrs Lizzie.
Little Vampie tried to sit quietly.
Mrs Lizzie left the block of flats. A **sunbeam** fell on her face, **dazzling** her.
Suddenly she heard dogs barking angrily. She heard shrill, angry **yapping**, and deep, furious **growling**.
Flocki and Bello again, thought Mrs Lizzie.
Then she was standing beside the dogs' **leads**, which were crossed over each other.
Mrs Maringer was hanging on to the end of one lead.
Mrs Anna was hanging on to the end of the other.
»That **brute** of yours snapped at my Flocki!« spat Mrs Anna.

sunbeam: der Sonnenstrahl; **dazzling:** blenden; **yapping:** das Kläffen; **growling:** das Knurren; **leads:** die Leinen; **brute:** die Bestie

»That **tyke** of yours attacked my Bello!« gasped Mrs Maringer.
Mrs Anna went red in the face. »Tyke? My Flocki is not a tyke! Look at the way your horrible creature is carrying on! I'm sure he's a mad dog. He ought to be reported.«
Mrs Maringer went **pale**. »A mad dog? We'll see who gets reported. You – you dreadful woman! Bello, come to your missus!«
Bello had no intention of coming to his missus. The dogs **prowled round in a circle**. The two women got the leads wound tighter and tighter around them.
»Your Bello has bitten my Flocki!«
»Your Flocki has torn my stockings!«
»Your Bello gets the stairs all dirty!«
»Your Flocki looks really **mangy**!«
»Mangy yourself, you nasty creature!«
»I won't be spoken to like that!«

tyke: der Köter; **pale:** blass; **prowled round in a circle:** liefen im Kreis; **mangy:** schäbig

Suddenly Flocki managed to break free. Next moment Bello broke free, too. Mrs Anna and Mrs Maringer screamed.
Flocki bared his teeth.
Bello **was drooling**.
A crowd of people had **gathered** round them.
»There's going to be a fight between those … er, those ladies,« said a little boy, rubbing his hands.
Mrs Lizzie felt a draught of air on her head. In the crowd she didn't see Little Vampie stinging.
She heard Mrs Maringer say, »Dear Mrs Anna, do you by any chance have time for a cup of coffee with me?« Her face was still covered with angry wrinkles, but her voice sounded sweet.
»Oh, yes, thank you,« said Mrs Anna. »I was

was drooling: geiferte; **gathered:** versammelt

going to ask you for your **eggnog** recipe, dear Mrs Maringer.« And the two of them walked away arm in arm.
Bello and Flocki ran ahead of them, carrying their leads in their mouths.
The crowd **scattered**.
»What a pity,« said the little boy.
Mrs Lizzie felt Little Vampie stretching out comfortably on her **bun of hair**.

eggnog: der Eierlikör; **scattered:** verstreute sich; **bun of hair:** der Dutt

A gentleman came up to her.
»Excuse me,« he said, »may I ask you a question? My name is Dr Obermeier. I am Chairman of the Board of the City Hospital, and Professor of Medicine at the university here.«
»What did you want to ask?«
»Did you see that insect just now? A moment before those two ladies so unexpectedly settled their **quarrel**, I thought I saw some kind of insect.«
Mrs Lizzie quite forgot to be cautious. »Insect?« she cried. »Oh, really! Did you hear that? He said you were an insect. And he calls himself a professor!«
»Who were you talking to just then?« asked Professor Obermeier.
Mrs Lizzie clapped her hand over her mouth.
Her knees were trembling.

quarrel: der Streit

Professor Obermeier was watching her closely. »Why are you afraid of me?« he asked in friendly tones.

»It's not that,« she said.

Professor Obermeier smiled. »You can tell me about it, don't worry. Anything you tell me will be **in confidence** between us.«

Suddenly Mrs Lizzie felt that her secret had been weighing on her mind for a long time. She wanted to tell someone else all about her Little Vampie and what he had been doing.

She raised her hat a little way. »Well, see for yourself!«

Professor Obermeier looked. Then he took a step backwards.

»That… that's a vampire!« he cried.

»He was only born a vampire,« Mrs Lizzie corrected him. »Now he's my Little Vampie. He has nothing to do with vampires, nothing at all. Anyway, vampires are only in stories.

in confidence: vertraulich

My Little Vampie is real. So he can't be a vampire, can he?«
Professor Obermeier was unable to answer this question.
He led Mrs Lizzie to a park bench.
They sat down.
Then he asked, »And how does your Little Vampie do that?«
Mrs Lizzie said **solemnly**, »He sucks the poison out of people's gall bladders.«
Professor Obermeier jumped up. »Sucks poison from their gall bladders? My good woman, do you know what you're saying?«
Mrs Lizzie stood up, too.
»I am not your good woman, and I know exactly what I'm saying. I may be old, but that doesn't make me stupid. We're going, Little Vampie!«
Professor Obermeier took her arm. He begged her not to be angry with him. »I'm

solemnly: feierlich

not quite myself,« he said. »Your Little Vampie could be of **unimaginable value** to **science**!«
His eyes sparkled at Mrs Lizzie like anything.
»Well, most of all my Little Vampie is of unimaginable value to our block of flats,« she said. »Since he arrived Hannes' mother hasn't hit him any more, and since she stopped hitting him he's been a different child. Only yesterday he carried my shopping basket upstairs for me! He's doing better at school, too. Right, so now we're off. Goodbye!«
Professor Obermeier **barred** her way.
»Don't you understand? You can't simply go away now. It would be pure **selfishness** to keep Little Vampie for yourself. He could be a **blessing** to all mankind!«

unimaginable value: der unvorstellbare Wert; **science:** die Wissenschaft; **barred:** versperrte; **selfishness:** die Selbstsucht; **blessing:** der Segen

»That's why we have to go. We have things to do.«
Professor Obermeier got more and more excited. **His voice was almost cracking**.
»What's more, sucking poison at random is strictly forbidden!« he cried. »Where would we be if anyone could suck poison where and when he liked? Do you know how long a

his voice was almost cracking: seine Stimme überschlug sich fast

doctor's medical studies take? And your Little Vampie hasn't even been to school, he hasn't taken any exams, he hasn't seen the inside of any university! No certificates, no diploma, nothing! And it's *your* responsibility!«
Mrs Lizzie nodded. »I'm happy with that.«
»But you can't stand in the way of progress!« Professor Obermeier was waving his arms about. »The human race is looking to you!«
All Mrs Lizzie saw was Professor Obermeier looking *at* her. She almost felt sorry for him. »But Professor,« she explained, »my Little Vampie doesn't need the human race. He can hardly manage all the poison and bile he meets anyway. Only yesterday he over-ate badly.«
The Professor **pounced** on that at once. »Then he may be ill, and he must come to us in his own interests! He can work with us and I'll look after him.«

pounced: hakte nach

»I can do that myself,« insisted Mrs Lizzie. »After all, I brought him up. And he's still far too young to work. There are laws against children working.«

Professor Obermeier **dismissed** the idea. »Only human children. Anyway, all that can be settled. And think of this – our hospital will get to be famous all over the world!«

»I couldn't care less.«

»And you'll be in the newspapers. And on television!«

»I couldn't care less about that either.«

Little Vampie lifted Mrs Lizzie's hat a little way and waved one wing. Professor Obermeier reached for him. Little Vampie howled.

»Stop that at once!« cried Mrs Lizzie.

Professor Obermeier let go. »I'm sorry,« he said with a slight bow. »I'm all confused. Such a thing has never happened to me before.«

dismissed: verwarf

Heavy at heart, Mrs Lizzie came to a decision.
»Very well, then. If it's really so important, he can go and live with you. But I'm coming, too.«
Professor Obermeier **beamed**. But then he said, »I didn't intend you to come with him.«
»I can come as a cleaning lady. I don't mind,« said Mrs Lizzie.
»I'm very, very sorry, but you're much too old to work for us.«
Mrs Lizzie shook her head. »If he's not too young then I'm not too old. Either with me or not at all.«
Professor Obermeier gave in.
But he insisted that Little Vampie must sleep at the hospital that night.
When Mrs Lizzie got home late that evening, her flat seemed to her terribly empty.

beamed: strahlte

Under a Glass Cover

Next morning Mrs Lizzie took the first tram to the hospital.
Little Vampie was **hunched up** under a glass cover that stood on a white table in a white room.

hunched up: zusammengekauert

There was a chair beside the table. A pretty young woman doctor was sitting on the chair. She was watching Little Vampie the whole time, and was writing down everything he did in detail.

Mrs Lizzie clasped her hands in the air above her head.

»Why is he sitting under that cheese-dish cover?«

Little Vampie hopped about excitedly and beat his little fists against the glass.

The young doctor wrote that down, too, and only then did she reply, in friendly tones, »On the Professor's orders.«

»But why?«

»Those were his orders,« repeated the doctor.

»Why?« repeated Mrs Lizzie.

The doctor shrugged her shoulders. »You don't ask a professor questions!«

»And I'm not asking if I can let Little Vampie out either,« said Mrs Lizzie.

Little Vampie flew up on her head and nestled into her bun of hair. »It's all right, my little one,« she said. »It's all right.«
But sad to say, it wasn't all right.
Professor Obermeier was very cross when he saw Little Vampie on Mrs Lizzie's head.
»This is totally impossible! A poison-sucker working for the city mustn't come into contact with dirt.«
Mrs Lizzie **took offence**. »Allow me to tell you that my hair is not dirty! It's freshly washed.«
Professor Obermeier explained that he didn't mean that kind of dirty. »It's a question of **germs** that might cause disease. They're everywhere.«
Little Vampie had to go back under the glass cover.
He hung his head.

took offence: war beleidigt; **germs:** die Krankheitserreger

He chewed the **tips** of his wings.
He didn't even look up when Mrs Lizzie tapped the glass.
»He'll soon get used to it,« said Professor Obermeier. »You wait and see.«
Mrs Lizzie hoped he was right.
But she didn't believe he was.
Little Vampie wasn't allowed to go on sucking bile out of people's gall bladders when they were angry.
He had to suck whatever poison Professor Obermeier said he must.
On his first day at the hospital Little Vampie sucked five different kinds of poison out of five different patients.
Professor Obermeier was delighted. He wrote letters to all the famous professors in the world, inviting them to his hospital. The patients were delighted, too. Although one man

tips: die Spitzen

screamed when he saw Little Vampie, and a woman fainted away.
»It would be a pity for him to suck nothing but bile and gall,« said Professor Obermeier. »His talents **would be stunted**.«
Little Vampie heard two people quarrelling in the corridor outside his room. And there he was under the glass cover and he couldn't do anything about it. He folded his wings over his head. That way no one could see him crying.
Mrs Lizzie felt like crying, too. But when

would be stunted: würden verkümmern

Professor Obermeier told her, »Little Vampie helped a man who was nearly dying today,« she was glad. But her heart was still heavy.
That evening Mrs Anna told her, »Just think, Mrs Lizzie, there was another car crash on our corner today. It was terrible, I can tell you. And we thought all that was better now. But there we are!«
Mrs Lizzie nodded sadly.
She heard the sound of a hard slap upstairs.
Next moment she heard Hannes crying.
And things were even worse next day.
When Professor Obermeier lifted the glass cover Mrs Lizzie was beside him. Little Vampie didn't look at her. He did what the Professor wanted. But he showed his sharp teeth and **hissed**. He'd never done that before.
Mrs Lizzie had to swallow, and then she had to swallow again.

hissed: fauchte

Her glasses **steamed up**. Cleaning them didn't help.
That evening Mrs Lizzie went to see Little Vampie again.
He was lying under his crumpled bat-wings.
Mrs Lizzie raised the side of the glass cover.
»It's me,« she whispered.
He didn't move.
»I'll sing you your song, shall I?« Her voice was trembling. »Then you'll sleep well.« She began humming:

steamed up: beschlugen

»Little Vampie wakes at dawn,
Rises bright and early ...«

He raised his upper lip and growled.
Mrs Lizzie couldn't get to sleep that evening.
She heard the church clock strike every quarter of an hour.
She heard the cars rushing by.
She heard her heart beating.
Next morning all her joints ached worse than they had ever ached before.
She went to the hospital and hurried to Little Vampie's room. Professor Obermeier was there already, bending over the glass cover.
Little Vampie had shrunk.
He was only the size of someone's middle finger.
Two days before he had been a whole inch longer.
»I'm taking him home,« said Mrs Lizzie.
»That would be the death of him,« said Professor Obermeier. »We must treat him here.«

The Professor **went to all sorts of trouble**.
Little Vampie was given **injections** and pills.
He was given a light diet and vitamins.
He was given sun-lamp treatment and **cod-liver oil**.
Nothing did any good. He went on shrinking.
His skin hung in folds round his thin body.

went to all sorts of trouble: gab sich alle Mühe; **injections:** die Spritzen; **cod-liver oil:** der Lebertran

Even his sharp **vampire fangs** were shrinking.

On the third day Professor Obermeier had to put on his strong reading glasses in order to see him at all.

Mrs Lizzie was shrinking, too. She didn't enjoy her food. She didn't even enjoy her coffee. She had to hold her skirt up with a belt or it would have dropped off. She was not just sad, she felt guilty, too.

»I never ought to have given in,« she kept saying. »I never ought to have given in.«

On her way home she saw Hannes, Klaus and Karin.

The three of them were **punching** Dieter in the stomach and asking, »What are you?« Then they answered their own question. »You're stupid.«

Mrs Lizzie took Hannes' shoulder and shook him. Hannes looked at her in surprise.

vampire fangs: die Vampirzähne; **punching:** schubsen

»Stop that at once!« said Mrs Lizzie. »At once!«
»I'll tell my Mum!« wailed Hannes.
Mrs Lizzie shook him again. »You do that. And tell her why I did it, too.«
»Makes no difference anyway,« said Hannes, with a **gloomy expression**.
Mrs Lizzie thought of the slap she had heard upstairs. She let him go.
Little Vampie, she thought, you ought to be here. What can I do? There's nothing at all I can do.
Hannes was standing in front of her, scuffing the toes of his shoes in the sand. She blew her nose. Then she invited the children to the ice-cream bar for an ice. All four of them.
The children were surprised.
Mrs Lizzie wanted to talk to them, but her voice sounded so miserable that she gave up the attempt.

gloomy: finster; **expression:** der Gesichtsausdruck

That night Mrs Lizzie dreamed of a gigantic vampire.

The gigantic vampire was standing by her bed and baring its teeth.

She woke up.

Her pillow was all wet.

Then she dreamed of a whole troop of vampires.

The troop of vampires was chasing her.

Their wings flapped like huge sails in a storm.
She woke up.
Her **nightie** was drenched with perspiration.
Finally she dreamed of the hospital.
She went into Little Vampie's room.

nightie: das Nachthemd

There stood the glass cover.
And there was nothing underneath it.
She woke up.
Her heart was beating so hard that it hurt.
Mrs Lizzie got out of bed.
The thoughts in her mind were **whirling about** in **confusion**.
Slowly, one of them emerged from the crowd.
Mrs Lizzie drank a cup of camomile tea and forced herself to think calmly.
By the time **dawn** was breaking above the buildings, she had made her decision.

whirling about: umherschwirren; **confusion:** die Verwirrung; **dawn:** die Dämmerung

The Last Chapter

Once again Mrs Lizzie took the first tram to the hospital. Feeling weak at the knees, she went into Little Vampie's room. He was still there.

But he was tiny.

As tiny as on the day she had found him in the cobweb.

»Little Vampie,« she whispered. »It's me. Please don't take fright. You mustn't take fright, do you hear?«

She picked up the glass cover and threw it on the floor, hard.

The broken glass **clinked** and **clattered**.
Little Vampie didn't move.
»You're not dead, are you?« whispered Mrs Lizzie. »You mustn't be dead! Please!«
A nurse came running in.
»What happened?« she asked.
Mrs Lizzie did not reply. She was bending over Little Vampie. She didn't know yet if he was still alive.
Bells rang. **Buzzers buzzed**. Lights went on and off. The door was flung open.
In came Professor Obermeier, followed by doctors and nurses and students.
»What happened?« asked Professor Obermeier.
Mrs Lizzie **straightened up**. »Nothing happened. I threw the glass cover on the floor **on purpose**.«

clinked: klirrte; **clattered:** schepperte; **buzzers:** die Summer; **buzzed:** summten; **straightened up:** richtete sich auf; **on purpose:** absichtlich

»On purpose?« The Professor tried not to shout. »You're putting him in danger! And medical experts on poison from all over the world are arriving tomorrow.«
»I couldn't care less about your medical experts. And he's been in danger ever since he was shut up here! He can't bear being shut up. As long as he was living with me and sucking poison out of people's gall bladders he was **bright as a button**. You've made him sick, Professor!«
»Are you out of your mind? People don't get made sick in my hospital!«
Professor Obermeier was getting angrier and angrier. »We gave him a chance to work for the good of the whole human race!«
Mrs Lizzie stroked the motionless Little Vampie with one finger. »It may be too late anyway. I ought to have taken him away

bright as a button: putzmunter

before. But you were so **bent on** getting to be **famous at his expense**!«

»That's an **insult**!« shouted Professor Obermeier. »Take it back at once!«

He took a step towards Mrs Lizzie.

At that moment the tiny vampire moved. He didn't really shoot through the air at the

bent on: versessen darauf; **famous:** berühmt; **at his expense:** auf seine Kosten; **insult:** die Beleidigung

Professor. He reeled through the air. But he stung into the Professor's gall bladder. Little Vampie was so weak that he had difficulty sucking, although after the first few gulps it worked better.
The doctors and nurses stared at the Professor.
Tears were running down Mrs Lizzie's cheeks.
Enormous surprise spread over the Professor's face.
Suddenly Little Vampie dropped off the Professor's stomach like a ripe apple.
Mrs Lizzie was only just in time to catch him before he fell to the floor.
He **curled up** in her hand.
»My dear Mrs Lizzie,« said the Professor, »I really didn't mean it that way.«
»That's all right,« she said. »Well, goodbye, then!«

curled up: rollte sich zusammen

»Oh, please do stay!« The Professor put his hand on her arm.
Little Vampie trembled.
»I'm sorry, Professor,« said Mrs Lizzie. »Little Vampie is still much too weak to be in hospital. He ought to be at home now. But you can bring your experts to see us if you like. I'll make you all coffee. And later, when my Little Vampie is better again, we'll come here if you need us. We like helping people. But no more **shutting** him **up**.«
»No more shutting him up,« repeated Professor Obermeier, and he nodded.
By now Little Vampie had climbed up on Mrs Lizzie's head.
»Don't pull my hair like that,« she said.
She smiled. If he was pulling her hair then everything was all right again. Or almost all right.
The doctors and nurses were still standing in

shutting … up: einsperren

a **semi-circle** around Professor Obermeier and Mrs Lizzie. They had difficulty closing their mouths again. They stood there like a silent chorus.
They just couldn't believe that someone had dared **to contradict** the Professor.

semi-circle: der Halbkreis; **to contradict:** widersprechen

Still less could they believe that the Professor would be so friendly when someone contradicted him.

»We must be going now,« said Mrs Lizzie. »We have a lot to do. Everything's been going wrong while he was here.«

She shook hands with the Professor. He walked her to the hospital gate, and the doctors and nurses followed.

Squeaking happily, Little Vampie pulled hairs out of Mrs Lizzie's bun. He waved to the Professor and the doctors and the nurses. The sun was shining.

»There now,« said Mrs Lizzie. »We'll just go home for today. I've earned a coffee, don't you think? But as soon as you're better again we'll go seriously looking. You know what I mean. One Little Vampie just isn't enough. We need lots of vampires like you!«

Mrs Lizzies Lieder

Lizzies Lied auf Seite 10/11

»In düstrer Waldesschlucht und alten Mauern,
Wo Füchse schleichen und der Uhu krächzt,
Da überkommt dich, Freund, ein kaltes Schauern,
Weil der Vampir nach deinem Blute lechzt.

Die schöne Adelheid von siebzehn Jahren
Ging einstens hin zum Walde ganz allein.
Es war ihr Liebster in die Welt gefahren,
Sie wollt' ihm eine Abschiedsträne weih'n.

Da hört' sie plötzlich eine Stimme sagen:
›Warum, o Mädchen, bist du so allein?
Ach, würde doch dein Herz für mich nur schlagen!
Du solltest eine Königin mir sein.

Ich würde dich in Samt und Seide kleiden,
mit Zuckerbrot und Wein dein Herz erfreun.
Und nie und nimmer würd' ich von dir scheiden,
wollt'st du mein Weib und meine Herrin sein!‹

Die schöne Adelheid, sie lauscht dem Werben.
Ach, Adelheid, wie ist dein Mund so rot!
Noch eh die Sonne sinket, musst du sterben,
liegst bleich und still im Moose und bist tot.«

Lizzies Lied auf Seite 45

*»Ja – so ein Vampir
ist kein böses Tier!
Muss es nicht sein,
wenn er von klein
auf Liebe spürt.*

*Mein Vamperl trinkt nur Milch und mag kein Blut
und macht die bösen Leute alle wieder gut.
Wenn einer tobt und schreit, was er kann,
dann flitzt mein Vamperl lautlos heran,
saugt ihm ein bisschen Gift aus der Gall' –
erledigt der Fall!
Mein Vamperl trinkt nur Milch und mag kein Blut
und macht die bösen Leute alle wieder gut.«*

Spottlied der Kinder auf Seite 47

*»Ri-ra-rum,
der Dieter, der ist dumm.
Ru-ro-rümmer,
der Dieter ist noch dümmer.
Der Dieter ist der Dümmste hier,
viel dümmer als ein Trampeltier.*

*Ri-ra-rum,
der Dieter, der ist krumm.*

Ru-ro-rümmer,
der Dieter ist noch krümmer.
Der Dieter ist der Krummste hier,
viel krummer als ein Trampeltier.«

Lizzies Lied auf Seite 56/57

»Morgens schon in aller Frühe
wird mein Vamperl munter.
Flitzt wie ein geölter Blitz auf die Straße runter.
Wo die Leute schimpfen, streiten
wegen lauter Kleinigkeiten,
wo sie raufen, fluchen, schrein,
dort mischt sich mein Vamperl ein.
Mein Vamperl trinkt nur Milch und mag kein Blut
und macht die bösen Leute alle wieder gut.
Wenn die Autofahrer rasen und die Leute wie die Hasen
jagen auf den Zebrastreifen, wenn sie miteinander keifen
und sich an die Stirnen greifen,
wenn man ringsum gellend hört
schaurig laut ein Hupkonzert,
wenn jeder tobt und brüllt, was er kann –
dann flattert heimlich mein Vamperl heran,
saugt ihm ein bisschen Gift aus der Gall' –
erledigt der Fall!
Da seht, wie es geht:

Die Streithähne fahren ganz friedlich weiter,
lachen und winken und grüßen sich heiter
und werden freundlich und wissen nicht wie
und sind zueinander nett wie noch nie.
Mein Vamperl trinkt nur Milch und mag kein Blut
und macht die bösen Leute alle wieder gut.«

Lizzies Lied auf Seite 91

»Morgens schon in aller Frühe
wird mein Vamperl munter,
flitzt wie ein geölter Blitz auf die Straße runter,
weil er ständig Leute trifft
voller Gift.
Doch wie fleißig er auch sticht,
das arme Vamperl schafft es nicht.
Er ist allein und viel zu klein,
es müssten viele Vamperln sein
für so viel Gift.
Ich denke mir mindestens acht oder zehn.
Wir beide sollten sie suchen gehn.
Wo immer sie sich auch heimlich verstecken,
wir beide werden sie sicher entdecken!
Zehn kleine Vamperln, wir bringen sie her,
dann hat mein Vamperl es nicht mehr so schwer.«

Hinweise zum Umgang mit der englischsprachigen Ausgabe

Liebe Eltern,
liebe Lehrerinnen und Lehrer,

diesem Buch liegt ein kommunikationsorientierter Ansatz zugrunde: Die Kinder sollen den englischen Text mit Freude lesen. Deshalb befinden sich am unteren Seitenrand Vokabelleisten, die Wörter bzw. Vokabeln, die über den in den Schulen üblichen Basiswortschatz der ersten beiden Lernjahre in der Fremdsprache hinausgehen, ins Deutsche übersetzen, und zwar mit der Maßgabe, dass die Angaben einfach an der entsprechenden Stelle beim Lesen in Gedanken eingesetzt werden können. Der Lesefluss soll möglichst wenig beeinträchtigt werden. Ganz bewusst wird in den Vokabelleisten daher z. B. auf das »to« zur Kennzeichnung eines Infinitivs verzichtet, konjugierte Verben auch jeweils in der entsprechenden Zeit übersetzt; so lautet die Angabe für »carried« daher »trug«. Wörterbuchähnliche Erklärungen, die auf Besonderheiten eines Wortes in Form, Flexion oder Tempus näher eingehen, sind keine unmittelbare Verständnishilfe. Ganz im Gegenteil: Sie würden an dieser Stelle die Lektüre mit zusätzlichen Hindernissen überfrachten und wären keine Erleichterung mehr.
Da Vokabelkenntnisse aber immer ein ganz individuelles Wissen sind, werden alle Kinder während der Lektüre feststellen, dass manches Mal Wörter erklärt sind, die ihm selbst ganz

einfach vorkommen, an anderer Stelle vielleicht eine Erklärung fehlt – hier gilt es, den Mut zur Lücke zu beweisen! Leseverständnis ist eine Fähigkeit, die sich trainieren lässt – auch dadurch, dass ein fremdsprachiger Text nicht immer Wort für Wort übersetzt werden muss, um verstanden zu werden. Schließlich schlagen wir auch in einem deutschen Text nicht jedes Wort nach, das wir nicht auf Anhieb begreifen.

Am Ende der Lektüre jedenfalls wird die Erfahrung, ein ganzes Buch auf Englisch lesen zu können, die Lesemotivation Ihres Kindes bzw. Ihrer Schülerinnen und Schüler kräftig steigern.

Birgit Hock

Birgit Hock ist Gymnasiallehrerin für die Fächer Deutsch und Englisch und arbeitet zurzeit als Sachbuchautorin und Journalistin. Sie hat zudem jahrelang an der Volkshochschule Englisch für Kinder unterrichtet und ist heute vor allem auf dem Gebiet der Lernhilfe tätig.